By **Alma Flor Ada** *Illustrated by* **Lori Lohstoeter**

SCHOLASTIC INC.
New York Toronto London Auckland Sydney
Mexico City New Delhi Hong Kong

ISBN 0-439-26774-9

12 11 10 9 8 7 6 5 4 1 2 3 4 5 6/0

Printed in the U.S.A. 14

First Scholastic printing, March 2001

The illustrations in this book were done in acrylics on illustration board.
The text type was set in Schneidler Medium.
The display lettering was created by Judythe Sieck & Tom Seibert.
Designed by Judythe Sieck

For Quica, gracias mil

—A. F. A.

For my godchild, Cameron Ivan Finkle. Love, Gomo

—L. L.

One summer morning Field Mouse set off to look for a friend.

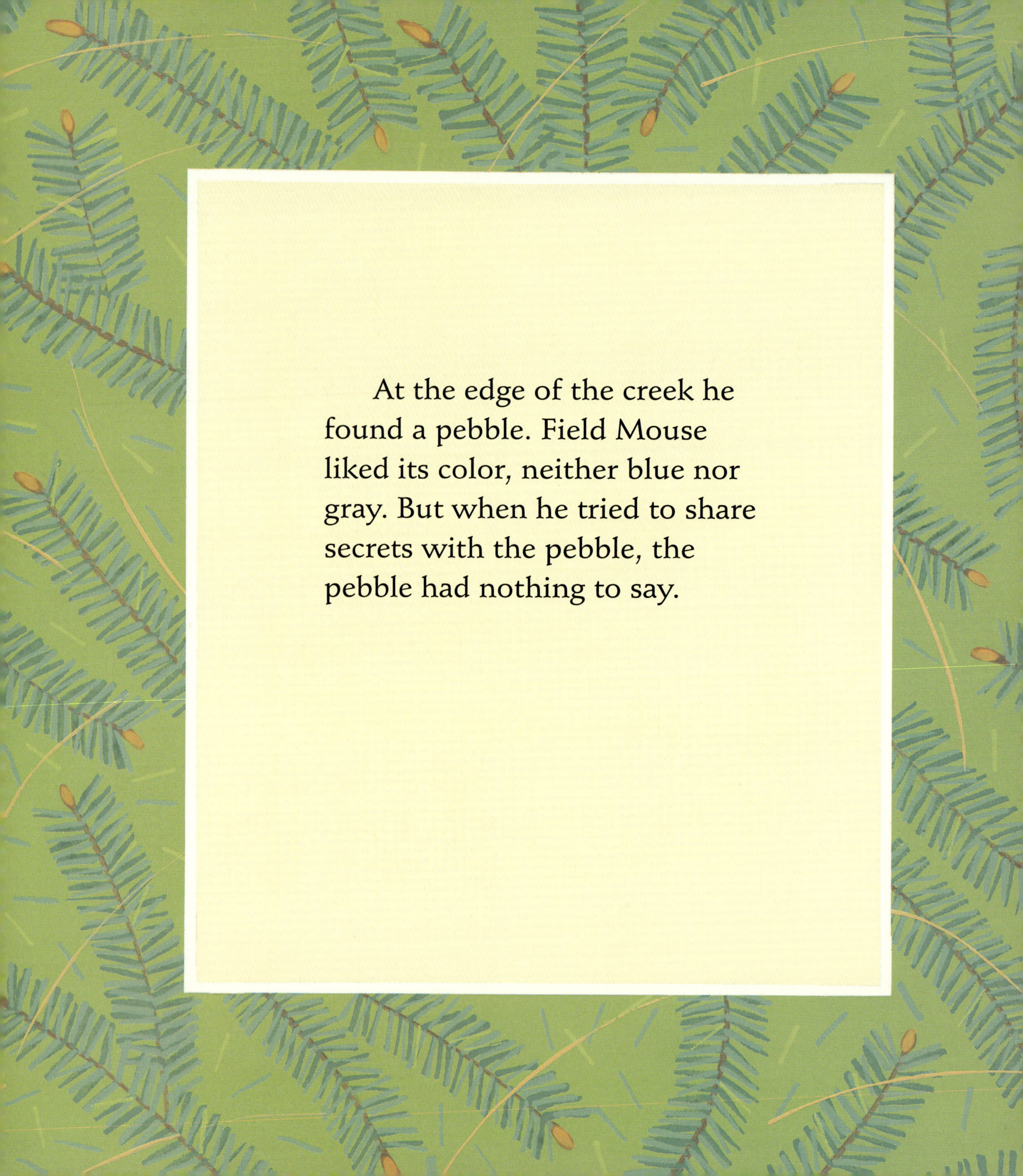

At the edge of the creek he found a pebble. Field Mouse liked its color, neither blue nor gray. But when he tried to share secrets with the pebble, the pebble had nothing to say.

Field Mouse scurried on a bit farther. Where the creek bent around the old willow tree, he noticed some tall grass swaying in the breeze. He liked the soft rustling sound of the wind in the grass, and he liked hiding among the stalks. But when he tried to tell the grass a secret, the grass only repeated its rustling sound.

Field Mouse left the grass behind and continued his search for a friend. He ventured farther than he ever had before. When he saw some cattails, he wondered if he was nearing the pond his grandfather had described to him in his stories. Suddenly he heard a curious sound—*croak, croak, croak.* Field Mouse wanted to see who dared to be so loud in the stillness of the warm afternoon.

Frog was sitting on a rock by the edge of the pond, croaking away. Field Mouse looked at Frog. He'd never seen anyone like her before. What beautiful big eyes she had! What a voice!

“Would you be my friend?” Field Mouse called out.

“Sure,” said Frog, “come croak with me.”

“I can’t croak,” said Field Mouse softly, “but I know some secrets.”

Frog was croaking so loudly, she didn’t hear him.

Field Mouse waited for a long while, enjoying the croaking. But when Frog jumped from her rock and disappeared beneath the surface of the pond, he scurried quietly home again.

That night Field Mouse kept thinking about Frog. How wonderful to have such a strong voice! Even if he could not croak like Frog, Field Mouse hoped they could be friends.

The following day Field Mouse returned to the pond. Frog was croaking happily on her rock. “Come jump with me,” she called when she saw Field Mouse.

Before Field Mouse could reply, Frog was jumping from rock to rock.

Field Mouse watched her disappear. He couldn’t jump so far or hop so high. He had hoped they could sit together and share secrets. But how wonderful to watch someone jump like that!

Field Mouse returned to the pond the next day. Even if he could not croak or jump, maybe he could still be Frog's friend.

"Come swim with me!" Frog called happily when she saw Field Mouse. She leaped into the water and swam across the pond.

Field Mouse couldn't swim. He was discouraged. *Maybe we just can't be friends,* he thought as he scurried home.

But the following afternoon Field Mouse came back to the pond once more. It was hard to give up the dream of such a friend. There was Frog, happily croaking on top of her rock. Field Mouse stayed hidden in the tall grasses, admiring Frog. What an extraordinary creature she was. How he wished he could croak, or jump, or swim so they could be friends.

Just then the ground around Field Mouse darkened. He knew well what that shadow meant.

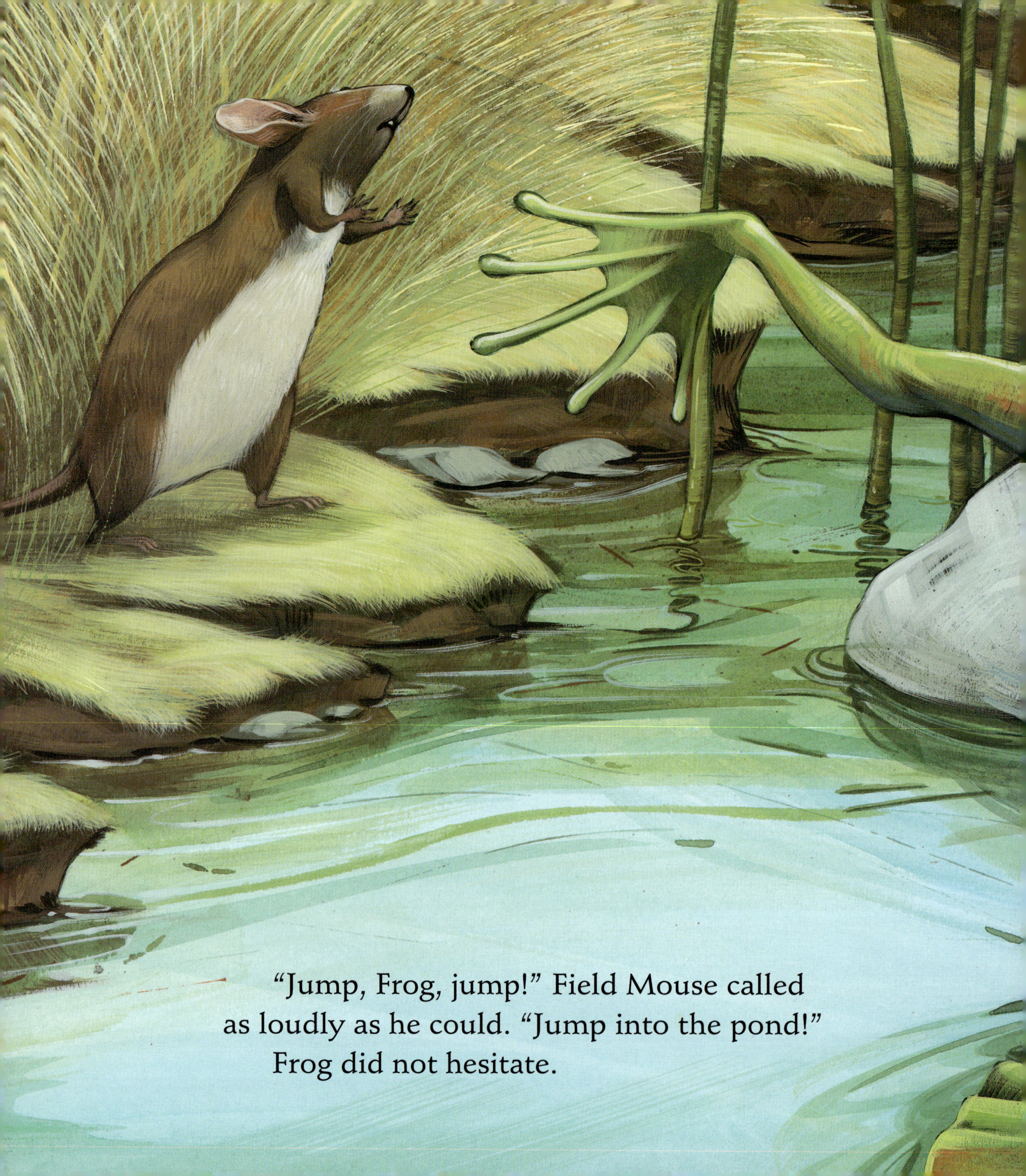

“Jump, Frog, jump!” Field Mouse called as loudly as he could. “Jump into the pond!”

Frog did not hesitate.

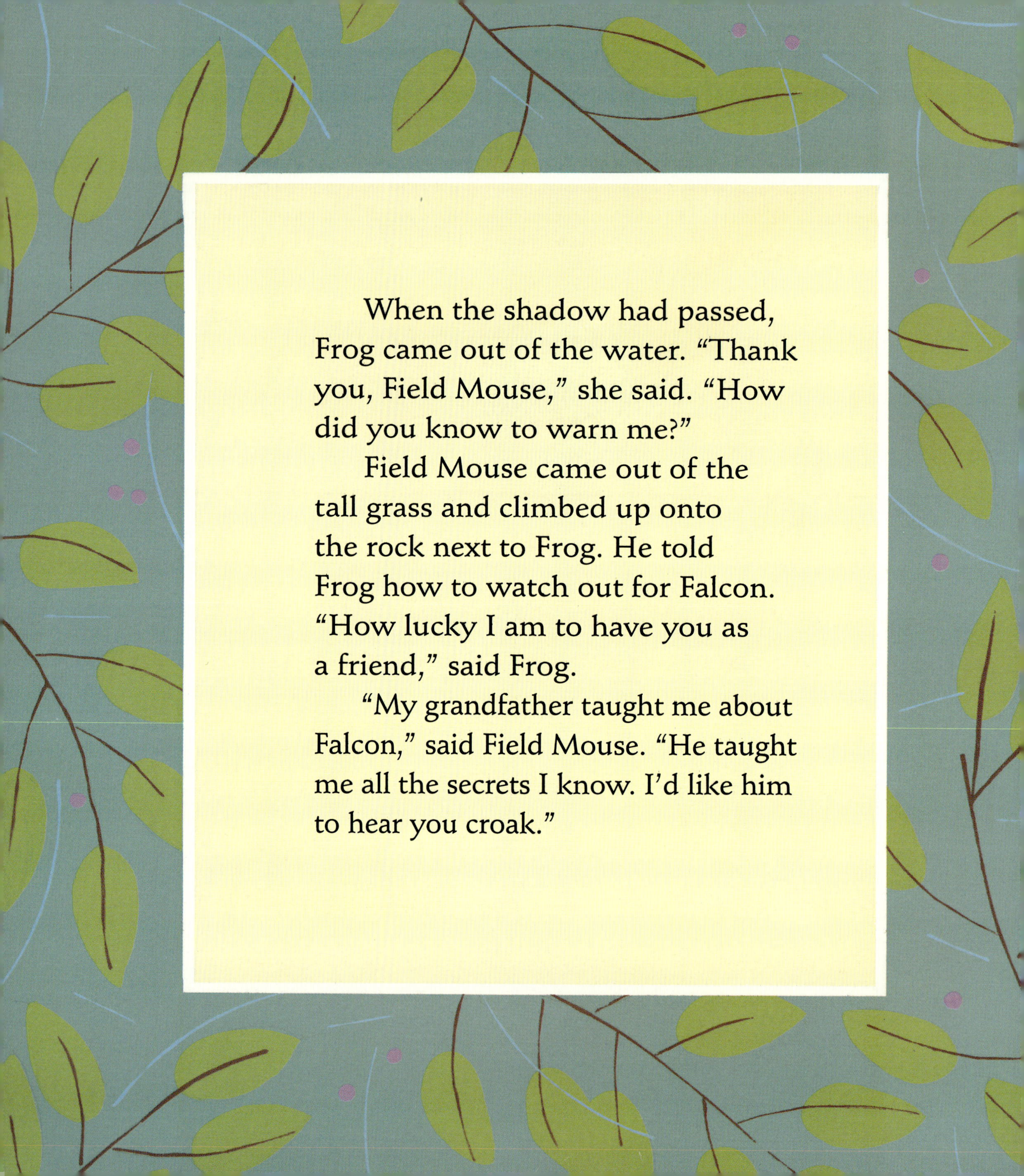

When the shadow had passed, Frog came out of the water. "Thank you, Field Mouse," she said. "How did you know to warn me?"

Field Mouse came out of the tall grass and climbed up onto the rock next to Frog. He told Frog how to watch out for Falcon. "How lucky I am to have you as a friend," said Frog.

"My grandfather taught me about Falcon," said Field Mouse. "He taught me all the secrets I know. I'd like him to hear you croak."

That night, when the moon rose from behind the mountains, Field Mouse and Frog sat together for a long, long time, listening to the old stories and secrets of the meadow and the pond.